GROUP MEMBER DISCUSSION GUIDE

8 Sessions

UNNAMED

Unsuspecting HEROES
Singled Out by God

CHRIS TRAVIS + NANCY KARPENSKE

Standard®
PUBLISHING

Cincinnati, Ohio

Published by Standard Publishing, Cincinnati, Ohio

www.standardpub.com

Copyright © 2010 by Standard Publishing

Also available: *Unnamed*, ISBN 978-0-7847-7439-7, copyright © 2010 by Standard Publishing

Printed in: United States of America

Project editor: Lynn Lusby Pratt

Cover design: Claudine Mansour

Interior design: Dina Sorn at Ahaa! Design

ISBN 978-0-7847-7440-3

15 14 13 12 11 10   2 3 4 5 6 7 8 9

CONTENTS

This guide is designed for small group use with the companion book *Unnamed*. It will help your group discuss the ideas from *Unnamed* and apply them in your lives. This happens best in groups that are growing together in real friendships, real faith, and real fun!

TRUE TO THE BIBLE

The aim is not to study a book however. It is to study God's Word, using *Unnamed* as a launching pad. We have designed this guide, like all the Standard Publishing products you've come to trust, to be true to the Bible.

TRUE TO LIFE

We designed this guide also to be true to life—life in the real world of friends, spouses, disappointments, kids, jobs, bills, and other everyday circumstances. We want this guide to help your faith intersect with other aspects of your life so you will live the life that Jesus promised: life to the full!

A number of features make this guide distinctive:

- *It is designed for busy people.* You will not need to spend hours preparing for meetings, whether you are the leader or another member of the group. However, reading the companion book *Unnamed* is highly recommended to help you get the most out of this study.
- *It is designed for people at various maturity levels.* You do not need to be a Bible scholar to facilitate or participate in these studies. The companion book will provide the teaching for each session. Your job is to discuss the truths from God's Word and apply them to your life.
- *It is designed to develop community.* Your group—whether you are a Sunday school class, Bible study, or small group—will grow closer to one another as you share your stories, study the Word, and serve together. The optimal number of participants in a group is usually about three to ten, depending on a variety of circumstances. But larger groups can still be very effective. We suggest you subgroup if your group is larger than twelve. You may want to break into several groups of three to six during the Study and Apply sections, for instance, for deeper discussion and more authentic application.

■ *It is designed to help you grow spiritually.* Real, lasting life change is the primary goal. The Holy Spirit will transform you as you allow him to work through God's Word and other group members to encourage, support, admonish, and pray for one another. Your group will employ Colossians 3:16: "Let the word of Christ dwell in you richly as you teach and admonish one another with all wisdom" (*NIV*).

HOW EACH SESSION IS ORGANIZED

Leader Preparation: This section is designed to prepare the leader's heart and mind for the meeting. To maximize opportunities for spiritual growth in your group, take time to read and reflect. Also use this time to pray for group members.

Bible Study Agenda: This study is designed to help participants *discover* truth from God's Word through group interaction rather than having the leader just *tell* them what it says. Participants will observe, contemplate, wrestle with, and take action on Scripture. Use the questions to facilitate lively interaction among group members. This will lead people to aha moments—when they *get it.* Ask follow-up questions to keep a good discussion moving. Keep the group on track with strong yet gentle encouragement and guidance.

FOR THE LEADER

You are in a vital position to help people grow in their relationships with God. The best leadership comes out of the overflow of a godly leader's heart. The Leader Preparation section and other leader helps are included to feed *your* heart first—to equip and encourage you before you lead your group. God has called you to shepherd this small group of people that he has entrusted to your care. We want to provide whatever support and resources we can to help you carry out this vital ministry to which God has called you. We have several resources available to help meet your needs. Please visit http://www.standard-pub.com/detail.aspx?ID=3194 to learn more about our small group help guides.

■ *Connect:* Utilize the Connect activities to help group members share about what they know best—themselves—and to get them actively involved in the discussion. Take advantage of these creative learning activities. The main question here is "What is *your* story?"

■ *Study:* These discussion questions are arranged to help members first observe and examine the Bible text, then understand and discern what the Scripture means and how they relate to it personally. The question here is "What is God saying to you in this passage?"

■ *Apply:* This is the most important meeting element. The leader should move the group toward this part of the process. Here they will relate God's Word to their own everyday lives and decide what they will *do* with it. The question here is "How will I respond?"

- *More Than Words:* Each session ends with a challenge for your group to take an action step that lives out the particular focus for the day. Some of these service opportunities are relatively simple, and others will take some additional planning. The question here is "How are we going to *reach others* with God's truth in a practical way?"

Before the Next Meeting: All group members should read the next chapter in *Unnamed* for the upcoming meeting. They may also look up Scripture passages if they like, but they do not need to do any other homework.

Leader's Between-Meeting Shepherding Ideas: A healthy, life-changing small group is more than just what happens during the meeting time. The leader should set an example by staying in contact with participants between meetings through phone calls, visits, e-mail, and personal letters or cards. The best groups are like close families that care for one another 24/7.

UNEXPECTED

2 KINGS 5:1-14

God prompts unexpected heroes to do the unexpected.

Expected: foreseeable, predicted, likely, considered probable or certain
Unexpected: unforeseen, not predicted, unlikely

THE BOTTOM LINE: We have to cultivate eagerness and awareness to recognize when God is moving in a way we don't expect or understand. We should expect the unexpected and be willing to jump right in.

THE GOAL OF THIS SESSION is to expand and refine our expectations of ways God can use us. We will evaluate our tendencies to continue in the same old rut, missing opportunities to be involved in the unexpected.

We will realign our vision to watch for "God moments."

We will commit to speaking courageously and showing kindness.

LEADER PREPARATION

Read 2 Kings 5:1-14 (and on through verse 19 for the rest of the story).

Read chapter 1 in the book *Unnamed* by Chris Travis.

Choose the activities and questions that best fit your group's style. Don't feel like your group must discuss every question.

You might decide to give out some gag prizes to those with the most unusual unexpected action in "Unexpected Turns" in the Connect section.

Bring some self-stick notes for question 11, enough for each group member to have two of them.

Pray that God will use you in unexpected ways as you facilitate this study.

CONNECT
Unexpected Turns

As you begin, the leader can have group members share their responses to the following questions.

■ Who has experienced some unexpected thing this week? Tell the group if you:

- Won something
- Got a raise
- Ran into an old friend
- Found something that had been lost
- Had a car break down
- Other _____

■ Who took an unexpected action this week? Was it something you've never done before? Something you've not done in the last year? In the last six months?

■ Who said something to someone this week that was out of the ordinary and unexpected? What was it, and what happened?

■ When was the last time you surprised yourself by something you said or did? (Or perhaps something you managed *not* to say or do?)

■ Based on the responses from members of your group, nominate one or two members as "most likely to take a risk," or "most likely to say or do the unexpected."

Kindness from a Stranger

Tell about a time when a stranger did some small or large kindness for you or someone in your family. Some possibilities include these: someone let you go ahead in line, gave up a seat for you, carried something heavy, stopped and changed your tire, or gave directions when you were lost.

How significant did this random act of kindness turn out to be for you?

___ Made me smile
___ Turned my day around
___ Reminded me God cares
___ Saved my life

STUDY

Read 2 Kings 5:1-14.

1. List from the text all the possible positive and negative traits about Naaman.

Positive	Negative

2. Why was Naaman highly respected by his king? Look for more than one reason. Who had given him success, and why do you suppose he would do that? (v. 1)

3. What did Elisha want Naaman to discover? (v. 8) What is significant about this?

4. Verse 11 in the *NASB*® reveals a peculiar comment by Naaman. He referred to himself as "the leper." What does this show about how he viewed himself? What do you think he could be feeling about taking the slave girl's suggestion that he seek healing from Elisha?

5. Read the rest of the story in verses 15-19. In what ways was Naaman's response to his healing unexpected? What did he do? Who went with him? What did he declare? How did this incident have greater impact than the slave girl might have anticipated?

LEADER'S NOTES

Ben-hadad was the name (or possibly title) of the Aramean king who tried to assist his army commander Naaman. Aramea is also known as Syria.

Elisha's command to go dip in the Jordan River involved a journey of at least twenty miles. (Source: James E. Smith, *I & II Kings* [Joplin, MO: College Press, 1975], 502.)

Elisha's message to the king of Israel was probably slightly sarcastic: there was more than one king who needed to recognize that there was a prophet in Israel.

6. This Bible story is full of ironic twists. Naaman shouldn't have been angry and bitter. The prophet was willing for him to be healed, but Naaman was not happy about the method. The girl *should* have been angry and bitter. She apparently wasn't. Suggest some possible reasons why the girl showed kindness to Naaman.

7. Read 1 Corinthians 1:27-29. How was this biblical principle lived out in Naaman's life?

ANOTHER UNEXPECTED HERO: MORDECAI

The slave girl's kindness to her captor, Naaman, is not the only example in Scripture of a behind-the-scenes person who did the unexpected. The star of the book of Esther is, of course, Esther. But her relative Mordecai was the one who started the chain of unexpected actions.

Read these verses and write Mordecai's unexpected actions in the space below:

___ Esther 2:21-23; 6:1-3

___ Esther 3:2-4

___ Esther 4:1, 2, 13, 14

Then match Mordecai's choices (below) with the actions in the Scriptures above:

A. Mordecai did the right thing sacrificially.
B. Mordecai did the right thing when he could have ignored a wrongdoing.
C. Mordecai did the right thing boldly.

APPLY

8. *This unnamed hero did what we might least expect. Instead of demanding justice, she offered grace.* (*Unnamed*, p. 20)

Have you ever been the recipient of grace when you deserved something less? Tell the group what you perceive as the possible motivation for the person who gave you kindness. Have you been very successful in offering grace to someone who has offended or hurt you? What has pushed you to act in an unexpected way in a tough situation?

9. Elisha's actions and command gave Naaman two choices: he could humble himself and be healed, or maintain his dignity and continue suffering from leprosy. Have you ever been given a choice that involved humbling yourself? How have your reactions been like Naaman's?

10. *Most days I do not expect to do anything more significant than I did the previous day.* (*Unnamed,* p. 15) How much does that statement ring true in your life? Suggest some small or large changes you could make that would cause you to raise your daily expectation quotient.

11. Read the following phrases:

- This week I expect to witness God doing something totally surprising.
- This week I plan to surprise my friends (and myself!) by speaking up, stepping out, and taking action.
- This week I will recognize my own rut and seek to rise above it.
- This week I will demonstrate kindness as a way of honoring the person who showed kindness to me.

Choose one or more of those phrases to jot on a self-stick note. Then display the note on your bathroom mirror or car visor. Let this jog your memory and activate your search for the unexpected.

12. *Hidden Potential,* a show on HGTV, takes house hunters to view homes that appear to be cramped and outdated. Then the designers reveal the hidden potential of the houses: how they can be remodeled and updated to become a dream home for the family.

Where are the sources of hidden potential in your life? (These might alter the course of your own life or someone else's.) Here are some possibilities:

- Try sharing something that brings you joy with someone who needs encouragement. Read a book together, visit your favorite park, or share a special dessert.
- Try something new. Offer yourself as a short-term volunteer in an area that you have never tried.
- Try saying something. Strike up a conversation with someone whom you ordinarily wouldn't talk to: a stranger at church, a clerk in a store, another parent at school. Offer a compliment or word of encouragement. If you feel tongue-tied, ask God for words to bless someone else's day.
- Try to take a small situation to the next level. Watch God get involved and develop the hidden potential.
- Try keeping a surprise journal: jot down the unexpected opportunities or challenges that God puts in your day.

MORE THAN WORDS

The eyes in your head will see just your daily routine. The eyes of your heart can notice the unexpected opportunities you have to act on God's behalf. (*Unnamed,* p. 28) Use the eyes of *your* heart and do the unexpected this week. Stick your neck out in the workplace by serving your coworkers. (If your workplace is your home, adapt the ideas to fit.) Go out of your way to choose people you normally might not serve. Here is a starter list. But remember Naaman's servant girl and feel free to be even more daring!

- Display a Thank You! or Good Job! poster for someone.
- Refill the candy container or the paper drawer in the copier.
- Wash the dishes in the office kitchen.
- Bring in afternoon treats.
- Do someone else's chore.

Before the next meeting read chapter 2 in *Unnamed.*

UNCLEAN
2 KINGS 7:3-11

God works through imperfect people.

Clean: spotless, pure, untainted, immaculate, perfect
Unclean: filthy, impure, dirty, contaminated, imperfect

THE BOTTOM LINE: Your past—no matter how ugly—will never keep God from using you.

THE GOAL OF THIS SESSION is to ignite in us excitement that God chooses to love and use imperfect people.

We will enlarge our view of God's grace and cleansing.

We will examine ways to overcome shame and move past guilt.

LEADER PREPARATION

Read 2 Kings 7:3-11.

Read chapter 2 in the book *Unnamed* by Chris Travis.

Pray for yourself and your group members to grow in faith that God wants to use you in spite of your flaws and failures.

For the Connect activity, prepare an opaque plastic container with lid (shoe box size). Attach a label to the top that reads "Hazardous Waste." Place inside the box several items of value (such as coins, candy bars, and gift cards for a free coffee). Cover the items with sand, leaves, or straw.

Are you aware of a group member who could share his story about overcoming shame? Contact that person early in the week in preparation for number 12. Ask if he would be willing to take three or four minutes to tell the group how God helped him move past shame and receive cleansing. Reassure him that he doesn't need to share all the "gory details." The point is to give the group a glimpse of the joy that comes from being set free from shame.

Plan to provide index cards for use in question 13.

Decide whether or not your group will celebrate Communion as suggested in the Apply section (number 14). If you plan to do so, ask a group member to bring grape juice and some kind of flat bread. Prepare a tray ahead of time.

CONNECT
Hazardous Waste

Everyone in the group should look at the box marked "Hazardous Waste." How would it feel if the refreshments for this session came out of that box? Not very appetizing, to say the least. How many in the group would be willing to stick a hand inside the box in order to claim a valuable prize? A few volunteers should retrieve a prize from the box. Afterward, discuss how it feels to rummage around in the "hazardous waste" in hopes of finding something of value.

Today we're going to discover who is contaminated and who is willing to take a risk to rescue and restore people who have been labeled "Hazardous Waste."

The Greatest Germ-O-Phobe

Who in your group could win the award for being the most paranoid about germs? What kinds of germ-ridden objects drive you crazy? On the leader's cue, raise your hand if this applies to you:

- I always wipe down the handle of the shopping cart before using.
- I open public restroom doors with my elbow.
- I use hand sanitizer in my workplace multiple times every day.
- I cringe when I have to touch a handrail in a public building.

STUDY

Read 2 Kings 7:3-11.

1. The men suffering with leprosy discussed two possible outcomes if they stayed at the city of Samaria and two outcomes if they went to the camp of the enemy (the Arameans). What were those outcomes? How would you state their odds?

LEADER'S NOTES

The Israelite king was named Jehoram. The Aramean king was still Ben-hadad, mentioned in the last session. Don't you wonder if Naaman was still the commander of the army?

People suffering with leprosy would have been breaking the law if they had entered the city. They had to stay outside the city.

2. Why couldn't the four men find anyone in the enemy camp?

3. What had the Arameans heard? What did they believe was happening? How did they react?

4. Name some of the things that the lepers found in the deserted camp. What did they do in the enemy camp?

5. What was the four men's motivation for returning to Samaria to announce the disappearance of the enemy army? (v. 9)

6. How did the gatekeepers react to the news they brought? (v. 11)

ANOTHER UNCLEAN HERO: THE SAMARITAN WOMAN

Read John 4:1-29.

1. Why was the woman surprised that Jesus asked her for a drink? (John 4:9)

2. What did Jesus know about the woman that had probably caused her to feel ashamed? (vv. 16-19)

3. What was the climax of the discussion about worship and the coming Messiah? (v. 26)

4. What evidence do you see that after her encounter with Jesus, the woman no longer carried a burden of shame and guilt? (vv. 28, 29)

APPLY

7. After filling themselves with food and drink and taking all the plunder they could manage to hide, the men with leprosy seemed to come to their senses. Have you ever had a similar experience, when you suddenly realized you had a responsibility to take action? Note it here, and share some of that experience with your group.

8. The four men suffered from mixed motives: they returned to the city to tell the good news because they feared punishment rather than because they wanted to help others. Have you ever suffered from mixed motives? How do you think God views mixed motives? What should a person do when he recognizes some selfishness in the midst of his desire to do the right thing?

9. God did not heal the four men of their terrible disease, but they still had a message to deliver. How does that idea compare with the way God works in our lives?

10. *None of our shortcomings disqualify us from God's redemptive work. In fact, sometimes it's through our weakness that God works most powerfully.* (*Unnamed*, p. 41) Suggest examples of how this has been true in your life or in the lives of Christians you know.

11. *My Amazing Renovation* is a show on HGTV that features over-the-top houses—huge, expensive, not your typical kind of home. The program usually tells a frustrating story of a makeover project taking more time and more money than the homeowner intended. In other words, the homes didn't start out as we see them now.

God is willing to be the contractor for an amazing renovation in each of our lives. He has unlimited resources, and is willing to pay out of his own pocket to give you the very best. Read these verses aloud in your group, and jot down a key thought for each. Check the passage that particularly speaks to you. Why did you choose that one?

____ Isaiah 43:19-21, 25

____ 2 Corinthians 5:17

____ Ephesians 4:24

____ Revelation 21:5-7

12. If the leader asked a group member ahead of time to share part of his story, that person can be introduced at this point.

13. Read aloud Lamentations 3:19-23. Think of the bitterness being the shame and doubt that bring paralysis. Now consider God's grace and forgiveness. *God can transform the dirtiest of us into one of his heroes.* (*Unnamed*, p. 41)

On the index cards that are distributed, each member should write this sentence and fill in the blanks: "I used to doubt that God would want to use me, because _____ , but now because of his grace I _____ ."

Carry your card in your purse or wallet this week where you will see it often.

14. If the leader has made arrangements, your group can share in a Communion service together.

Each of us was raised in a world hopelessly marred by sin. Each of us contributed to the brokenness by making our own sinful decisions. (*Unnamed*, p. 40) Have someone read 1 John 1:7-9. Every time we eat the bread and drink the cup, we are reminded that the price has already been paid to purify us from all sin. We celebrate cleansing and forgiveness!

MORE THAN WORDS

We typically don't encounter people suffering from leprosy on the streets of our communities. In our era, however, people with mental illness are often treated as if they have leprosy. Contact a mental health center in your community. Ask about ways your group could make a difference in the lives of some of their clients.

The mentally ill are often the most likely to be homeless. Perhaps your group could collect socks or small calendars to give away. Have each group member bring a friendship or encouragement card to give with your other donations. Small gestures may not seem heroic, but they make an impact and say, "Someone cares about you."

Before the next meeting read chapter 3 in *Unnamed*.

UNPOLISHED

LUKE 2:1-20

The power is in the message, not the messenger.

Polished: smooth, cultured, refined in manners, perfected
Unpolished: rude, coarse, rough

THE BOTTOM LINE: *Untrained and unpolished—but utterly genuine—people, simply prepared to gently and respectfully talk about their relationship with God, will best connect with people today. (Unnamed, p. 51)*

THE GOAL OF THIS SESSION is to realize that polished presentations of faith are not required—the important thing is to become at ease in sharing our faith.

We will evaluate our personal listening skills and plan improvements.

We will practice the ten-sentence approach.

We will prepare a simple three-minute testimony.

LEADER PREPARATION

You'll need approximately 23 index cards for question 7. Using a felt-tip pen, print one of these words or phrases on each card: Bible, God, Creator, Ruler, Love, Justice, Humans, Sin, Rebellion, Separation, Grace, Savior, Jesus, Son of God, Sinless, Sacrifice, Death, Resurrection, Faith, Repentance, Baptism, New Life, Holy Spirit.

If you choose to do "Good News/Bad News" in the Connect section, you may want to provide small prizes for the winning team.

Read Luke 2:1-20.

Read chapter 3 in *Unnamed* by Chris Travis.

Pray that you won't be ho-hum about a familiar Bible story. Ask God to help you and your group to view this topic with fresh eyes.

CONNECT

Choose one of these opening activities.

Best News Ever

- When was the last time you called a friend to tell him or her some great news? What was it? Who did you call? How many calls did you make to spread the word?
- When was the last time you struck up a conversation with a stranger? What motivated you? What did you talk about?
- Besides the news about Jesus' love, what is the greatest piece of news you've ever received? Who delivered the news? How did the person tell you?

Good News/Bad News

Imagine that you get a phone call. The caller says, "Which do you want first, the good news or the bad news?" Divide into two teams. Brainstorm for two minutes a list of both bad and good topics that the caller could be waiting to tell. For instance, a credit card company is calling to say your identity has been stolen. Or Publishers Clearing House is calling to say they can't find your house, but you have won. The team with the most suggestions wins. (If teams propose similar or identical ideas, those cancel each other out.)

STUDY

Read Luke 2:8-20.

1. Imagine that you have never heard this story before. What stands out to you? What questions emerge?

2. What emotions do you sense in these shepherds during the different scenes?

LEADER'S NOTES

The average citizen in Bible times looked down on shepherds. The youngest son of a landowner often became the shepherd for the family flock. (Remember David?) Shepherds were the bottom rung of society, along with tax collectors—only they smelled worse. You can read more in a brief article, "Shepherd's Status," by Randy Alcorn, posted in Articles about Holidays, at Eternal Perspective Ministries, http://www.epm.org/artman2/publish/holidays/Shepherd_s_Status.shtml.

3. Suggest what Bethlehem residents might have said the next morning after being awakened by the shepherds exuberantly telling their good news.

4. Suggest what the shepherds might have talked about as they ate breakfast the next morning back at their sheepfold.

ANOTHER UNPOLISHED HERO: PAUL

Read 1 Corinthians 2:1-5.

1. We think of Paul as a powerful speaker, well trained in the "College of the Pharisees." He wrote about himself in these verses with very humble words. What did Paul say that he lacked in speaking ability? (1 Corinthians 2:1)

2. What pitiful credentials did he mention in verse 3?

3. Why didn't it matter to Paul that his message didn't come across as very polished? (vv. 4, 5)

4. In your opinion, was Paul's speaking in Corinth truly unpolished? What point was he really trying to make by indicating that it was?

See also 2 Corinthians 3:4-6. Consider this opinion: "Usually heroes are admired only from a distance, not when they are doing their great work. In their own time they were often regarded as fools or failures." (Source: Ajith Fernando, *The NIV Application Commentary: Acts* [Grand Rapids, MI: Zondervan Publishing House, 1998], 381.)

APPLY

5. *The people were astonished, quite simply, because the power was in the message, not the messenger. (Unnamed, p. 54)*

Why is it significant that God chose shepherds to receive the birth announcement? How have you seen God use individuals even when they felt inadequate?

6. Tell about a time when you attempted to share your faith but ended up feeling like you said the wrong thing. How did you recover from the embarrassment of being unpolished? Did you study up to do better next time? Did you pray like crazy that God would make something good happen from your feeble attempt? What intimidates you about talking about your faith?

7. If you had only ten key words or phrases to convey God's message of salvation through Jesus, which ten would you choose? Look at the key words and phrases on the index cards the leader prepared. Choose the ten that flow best for you, and jot them down here. If time permits, add a sentence of explanation to each word. Then pair up with a partner to share and discuss the choices.

8. *Real Simple* is a popular magazine that features articles about making home, life, and work more manageable. It includes many practical tips through the "Simply Stated" blog and the "Keep-It-Together Check-list."

One of the real simple ways to share your faith is to use only three minutes to say what you have to say. Practice sticking to the very simple by completing these sentences:

My life before Jesus . . .

I met Jesus . . .

My life since Jesus . . .

9. *Life with this God is like a never-ending sense of relief.* (*Unnamed*, p. 55) Do you think most Christians feel this way about God? Why or why not? How would having this attitude change the way that we share our faith with others?

10. Evangelism isn't about selling an idea. Christians have realized how crucial it is to build a relationship first, by listening to the person with whom you want to share. How would you rate your listening skills? What would your spouse or friends say about your listening skills? What advice would you give to someone who wants to improve his ability to listen to a nonbeliever's story?

MORE THAN WORDS

Here's an idea to celebrate the good news of Jesus' birth even though Christmas may be months away. Call your local pregnancy center. Ask about the needs of their clients. In honor of Jesus' birth, choose some practical ways to help expectant mothers.

Most pregnancy centers are always in need of maternity and baby clothing. Have each member of your group bring a package of disposable diapers to donate. Or you could throw a baby shower for an expectant single mother. Each family in your group could bring some baby items. Package them all up in a bassinet or a baby bathtub.

Before the next meeting read chapter 4 in *Unnamed*.

UNWORTHY

MATTHEW 8:5-13

God gives us direct access to him.

> **Worthy:** having value, important enough, having desirability or significance
> **Unworthy:** good for nothing, useless, lacking value, contemptible

THE BOTTOM LINE: God has an open-door policy. Jesus is the door. *Unworthy* has been erased from any description of those who call Jesus their Lord.

THE GOAL OF THIS SESSION is to reduce our feelings of unworthiness by realizing that our value comes from God through Jesus.

We will get a bigger picture of God, stand in awe of him, and be overwhelmed by his compassion.

We will respond to God's open-door policy by ramping up our prayer lives.

Read Matthew 8:5-13.

Read chapter 4 in the book *Unnamed* by Chris Travis.

Review the number 15 prayer activity under the Apply section. Contact a group member who feels comfortable leading your group in prayer. Turn him or her loose on preparing the suggested prayer ahead of time.

Pray that you and your group will increase both your understanding and your practice of direct access to God.

CONNECT
Locked Out

■ Have you ever been locked out of somewhere you needed to be, like your car or the store where you were supposed to pick up your wedding dress? Tell your group the story of how you gained access.

■ Have you ever been denied access to someone whom you really needed to talk to? Your doctor? Your child's principal? A manager at work? What worked and didn't work as you attempted to get your message through? Tell your group how you managed your frustrations and tried to maintain a Christian attitude while gaining access.

Mother, May I?

The childhood game Mother, May I? is really all about keeping the contestants from getting too close to the "mother" running the game. Play an abbreviated version to remind your group of the futility of trying to get close. Appoint someone to be the mother. Line up the contestants at the opposite end of the room. Players should take turns asking the mother if they may approach. Usually the dialogue goes something like this:

"Mother, may I take ten baby steps?" The mother replies something like, "No, but you may take six steps." If the player moves before repeating the question "Mother, may I?" then that move is cancelled. The game includes steps such as frog leaps, ballerina twirls, scissors steps, and others your group might remember or invent. Players hope to distract the mother so that she won't notice someone getting too close who can then take her place.

This child's game reminds us that we can't make up our own steps or our own list of must-dos to get close to God on our own terms. What are some ways in which people who don't understand God's grace try to get God's attention?

STUDY

Read Matthew 8:5-13.

1. Why did the centurion come to Jesus? What did the centurion evidently *believe* about Jesus, not necessarily *want* from Jesus?

2. *This Roman soldier . . . wasn't so bold simply because he didn't understand who Jesus really was. He was bold because he* did. (*Unnamed*, p. 68) Speculate about how the centurion came to his belief in Jesus. What do you suppose he had heard or seen while stationed in Capernaum? What do you learn about the town from these verses?

Matthew 4:18

Mark 2:1-12

Mark 5:22-43

Luke 4:31-37

Luke 7:1-5

3. What did the centurion believe that he had in common with Jesus? What differences did he recognize existed between them?

4. Why was Jesus amazed ("astonished," *NIV*)?

5. Who will be present in the kingdom of Heaven? With whom will they get to have dinner? Where will the dinner take place? (v. 11; see also Isaiah 25:6-9; Matthew 22:1-14)

6. What did Jesus say was lacking in the people of Israel? According to verse 12, what will the result be for them?

LEADER'S NOTES

Capernaum was located on the northwestern coast of the Sea of Galilee. You may want to flip to the back of a Bible and locate this on a map of Palestine during Jesus' ministry.

Jesus was "amazed" only one other time in the Gospels, in Mark 6:6—and in a negative way rather than a positive one.

The parallel account of this incident is recorded in Luke 7:2-9. Review this passage and note additional background about the centurion.

ANOTHER UNWORTHY HERO: JOHN THE BAPTIST

1. How did John compare himself to Jesus in John 1:15?

2. How did John describe himself in John 1:23?

3. How did John describe himself in John 3:29? What emotion did he have when hearing Jesus?

4. In John's estimation, who had more power? What did he consider himself unworthy to do? (See Mark 1:7.)

5. When Jesus came to be baptized by John, what was John's response? (See Matthew 3:14.)

6. How did John summarize the future for himself and for Jesus in John 3:30?

7. What would it look like for you to apply that verse to your life? How could you allow Jesus to increase and your own (*fill in the blank*) to decrease?

8. What opinion did Jesus have about the worthiness of John the Baptist in Matthew 11:11?

APPLY

7. What about God astonishes you the most: his creation, his gift of Jesus, his power to change people today, his unfailing love toward you, or some other facet of his works or character? Based on the amount of time you spend talking to God about one of these aspects, what would your answer be?

8. What activities do you include in your schedule that remind you of God's greatness and love? Number these according to the importance you give them (1 being most important).

___ Spend time in nature
___ Spend time listening to music
___ Spend time reading
___ Spend time meditating on Scripture
___ Spend time in corporate worship
___ Spend time _____

Compare your choices with others in your group.

9. *Sometimes when people would ask me to pray for something, I'd get this sense that they thought God would be more inclined to do something for them if I asked him to, like I had a direct line or something. I do have direct access, but there's nothing special about it at all. You do too. (Unnamed, p. 69)*

Fans who want to keep up with the daily lives of movie stars watch the TV show *Access Hollywood*. In reality, true access is extremely limited. Those who watch the show are treated to celebrity photos and the latest gossip. How does this "fake" access contrast with the true access believers have to God?

10. Do you have a prayer *time* or a prayer *life*? How would you evaluate your prayers? Would you rate them to be representative of the powerful and magnificent God you love and serve? How so?

11. Do you commonly pray the "if only" prayer, afraid you will annoy God if you ask too much, so you ask too little? If so, how could you overcome that tendency?

12. Do you often pray the "somehow" prayer, as if your request is so complicated and so unlikely that it might be out of God's capability? If so, how could you overcome that practice?

13. Are your prayers heavily weighted with personal information, requests, and even advice for God . . . and frequently lacking in praise of God's character, apart from what he does for you? If so, how could you improve this?

14. *There, rocking in the surging tide, I became aware of the presence of this being who tells the ocean what to do. The ocean could erase me, but God could erase* it. *What an unimaginable God, powerful beyond comprehension. I opened my mouth to pray . . . and then shut it.* Who am I to speak to this God? *I felt, in a word, unworthy. (Unnamed,* p. 65)

When's the last time you stood silent before God, speechless, acknowledging that you don't have words impressive enough to praise and thank him? What would you change to honor God in a greater way in your prayers? How will you implement that change this week?

Note: *Pray with Purpose, Live with Passion: How Praising God A to Z Will Transform Your Life* by Debbie Williams (Howard Publishing, 2006) is a great resource for revamping your prayer life. If your group is comprised of teens, you might want to consider *Praying from the Gut* by Steven James (Standard Publishing, 2004).

15. Read these verses about the direct access believers have to God.

> Ephesians 2:13
> Hebrews 4:16
> Hebrews 10:19
> James 1:5, 6
> James 4:8

Then write a prayer thanking God for removing barriers that keep us at a distance from him. If the leader has assigned this activity to a group member ahead of time, that person can use his or her prepared prayer to lead the group in prayer.

MORE THAN WORDS

Access is something homeless people seldom have. Consider collecting funds from your group to purchase some phone cards. If you don't know where to find homeless people in your community, drop off the cards at the police station or a place that serves meals to the homeless. These cards will help individuals contact their family members or check on job opportunities.

Before the next meeting read chapter 5 in *Unnamed.*

UNDERESTIMATED

─── JOHN 6:1-15 ───

God can do more through you than you can imagine.

> **Estimate:** to place value, to judge the value of an item or person, to take the measure of something
> **Underestimate:** place low value on, less than calculated, undervalue, discount

THE BOTTOM LINE: When God is in the equation, the sum is always exponentially greater than facts or logic would dictate.

THE GOAL OF THIS SESSION is to focus our thoughts on the immense capabilities of God, then respond appropriately.

We will celebrate God's power and willingness to multiply our offerings to him.

We will recognize that God's "performance record" makes it possible for us to attempt big things on his behalf.

We will seek ways to be more willing to get personally involved in serving God by serving others.

LEADER PREPARATION

Read John 6:1-15.

Read chapter 5 in the book *Unnamed* by Chris Travis.

Pray about your own tendency to underestimate the potential of your contribution as facilitator of the discussion. Ask God to help you focus on your part—the preparing and praying. Ask God to use you to fulfill his purposes in your group.

Provide index cards for question 12.

CONNECT
What We Have Here Is a Failure to Calculate!

"Jesus, do you see how many people are here? What are you thinking?" Jesus' disciples were positive that he had miscalculated.

■ Can you remember a time when you made a mistake in your planning and miscalculated something? Were the results funny, disastrous, or embarrassing? Perhaps you:

- Planted too many zucchinis in a small space
- Prepared a dinner for guests and ran out of food
- Bought a yard of fabric or a roll of wallpaper and needed twice as much
- Underestimated how long it would take you to drive to an important meeting
- Missed how much it would cost for your kids to go to college—by a long shot!

■ Discuss the impact of your mistake. Did it cost you beyond feeling bad about yourself? How did it cause you to be more cautious in your next venture?

Jesus' disciples had been eyewitnesses to many of Jesus' amazing works. But when he purposely presented them with a new challenge, they could see only the size of the problem, not the power of their leader.

Oversize Request

■ Share a time when you believed God was telling you to do something that you felt was way out of your comfort zone or your capability. Did you resist, or obey? How did it turn out?

■ Tell about a small thing you once did for someone that turned out to be a big deal from the other person's point of view.

STUDY

Read John 6:1-15.

1. What did John record about why the crowd followed Jesus?

2. In your opinion was Philip cynical and skeptical, or was he sincere in his answer to Jesus? Support your answer.

3. Why do you suppose Jesus told the disciples to gather up the leftovers? What is the significance of the twelve baskets of leftovers? Try to suggest more than one possibility.

LEADER'S NOTES

Immediately before this day of teaching, healing, and feeding the people, Jesus and his disciples had received the tragic news of the beheading of John the Baptist. They took a boat across the Sea of Galilee to get away from the crowds and have some private time (Mark 6:31).

It was late afternoon, early evening. The crowd had been listening to Jesus all day (Matthew 14:15).

The people were organized into groups of hundreds and fifties for the distribution of the food (Mark 6:39, 40).

Luke 9:16 gives the best snapshot of Jesus praying over the boy's lunch before it was distributed.

4. This is the only miracle besides the resurrection of Jesus that is recorded in all four Gospels. Why do you think the writers all emphasized this miracle? What makes it more significant than Jesus' raising individuals from the dead or stopping the storm?

Read Luke 9:13.

5. What challenge did Jesus give the disciples? Why do you suppose he did that? What response do you think he might have wanted from them?

Read Mark 6:35-38.

6. How do you imagine Andrew found the boy and his food?

 ANOTHER UNDERESTIMATED HERO: _____

Use these clues to discover the hero:

- His nemesis looked small to him in comparison to the size of his God.
- He refused to wear the king's armor.
- His opponent called him a dog.

Read 1 Samuel 17:25-51.

1. What shocked him about the Israelite army? (1 Samuel 17:26)

2. What shocked the king about his offer? (v. 33)

3. Why did this person know he would be successful? (v. 37)

4. What did he use for a weapon (v. 40), and how did he approach the fight? (v. 48)

5. What was the outcome of the fight? (vv. 49-51)

6. What did this underestimated hero have in common with the young boy in John 6?

APPLY

7. *Buying food for so many was simply out of the question. Philip sounded a little shocked by Jesus' request. "Even if we worked for months, we wouldn't have enough money to feed them!" (v. 7). Not exactly a huge vote of confidence in Jesus, but who could blame him? (Unnamed, p. 80)* When was the last time you "pulled a Philip"? You had seen God do amazing things, but you faced a tough situation and said, "There's no way we can pull this off." Did your prediction come true, or had you underestimated God? What happened?

Read Psalm 95:9, 10.

8. How did God feel about the children of Israel? Why? How was their attitude similar to Philip's? How does seeing God's displeasure with the Israelites challenge the way you express your trust in God when you are facing a big obstacle?

9. When was the last time you "pulled an Andrew"? You didn't really have a clue about how to solve the current problem, but you took what was in your hand (or heart or mind) and turned it over to Jesus? What was the result? How did God surprise you?

10. *Often when we underestimate ourselves, we actually underestimate God. You never know what Jesus may do—what may follow the "then Jesus"—in response to a tiny act of obedience, generosity, or kindness on your part. God can do more through you than you imagine, so don't ever let the apparent smallness of a gesture give you pause. (Unnamed, p. 85)*

Elaborate on the "then Jesus" theme. Recall several precarious or hopeless situations in your life that turned around with a "then Jesus" moment. Does it surprise you to consider that underestimating your abilities and potential may actually be underestimating God? Why or why not? Suggest some tangible ways in which you could begin to overcome your lack of confidence.

11. Brainstorm a list of small, insignificant roles you notice in your daily life (taking out the trash, making the coffee at work, saying hello to someone in the hallway, folding the laundry, making eye contact with the checkout clerk . . .). In your group, talk about possible ways to act as God's person, bringing his purposes into that small action. Choose one of those roles to throw yourself into during the upcoming week. Ask God to multiply the impact of your seemingly small action.

12. Read these Bible verses about God's power. Choose one to write out on an index card. Keep the card where you can see it throughout the week.

Psalm 138:8
2 Corinthians 1:9
2 Corinthians 9:8
Hebrews 7:25
Jude 24

13. *Every character propels the drama. If an actor decides to give something less than 100 percent because he feels his role is too small, the whole show suffers. It can weaken the entire storyline if anybody refuses to take a role seriously.* (*Unnamed*, p. 84)

In the theater world, the greenroom is a backstage location where performers wait until it is their time to go on stage. In life, however, believers do not always know when they will be called, nor do they know if the part they will play is a leading role or a minor character. In your group, brainstorm some possible actions and attitudes that God desires from his troupe of actors. Check out these Bible verses for some hints. We should *always* be prepared to:

John 8:29

Acts 24:16

Philippians 4:4

1 Thessalonians 5:15

1 Peter 3:15

MORE THAN WORDS

"What's in your wallet?" has been a popular advertising slogan for a credit card company. They want you to feel powerful and confident because with their card you have "unlimited resources." Look at the other extreme: the coins in your pocket. They seem nearly worthless. What could your group do by collecting and pooling your change? Challenge the group to save their change and bring it to the session for each of the three remaining weeks of the study.

Appoint two group members to come up with two possible charitable ways to use the collection. One idea is to purchase movie or zoo tickets for a single-parent family.

Before the next meeting read chapter 6 in *Unnamed*.

UNCERTAIN

MARK 9:14-27

God desperately wants to help us believe.

Certain: assured in mind or action, sure (especially on the basis of objective evidence), reliable, guaranteed
Uncertain: doubtful, questioning, indefinite, not reliable

THE BOTTOM LINE: My uncertainty does not stop God from coming to my aid.

THE GOAL OF THIS SESSION is to encourage each other by sharing ways that each person has dealt with and moved through uncertainties.

We will reexamine God's commitment to run toward us in our doubts.

We will commit to continuing to reach toward God in faith.

LEADER PREPARATION

Read Mark 9:14-27.

Read chapter 6 in the book *Unnamed* by Chris Travis.

For the first Connect activity, bring a small toolbox with the following equipment: an instruction manual, a pair of pliers, a roll of duct tape, a pair of protective goggles.

Check out the lyrics of the song "Never Been Unloved" by Michael W. Smith and Wayne Kirkpatrick, ©1998 Milene Music. Visit www.christianlyricsonline.com. You may want to print out the lyrics for the group or bring a laptop to the session and look up the song at that time. These lyrics are referenced in question 11.

Talk with God about your own journey in and out of uncertainty. Ask him to help you recall ideas or people who helped you, so that you can encourage others.

CONNECT

Choose one of the three options below to begin thinking about today's topic.

Essential Tools

Imagine that you could purchase a toolbox filled with equipment for dealing with and overcoming doubt. What tools would you expect to find? What has worked in your own faith journey when you experienced uncertainty?

Examine the contents of the toolbox the leader brought and suggest how each item could symbolize a way to positively deal with uncertainty. For example, the instruction manual could represent the Bible. We could get instruction from God about dealing with our doubts. Suggest other tools that could be used.

Living with Uncertainty

Review the statements below. Assign one of the four categories of certainty to each of the statements.

	POSITIVELY NO	NOT SURE	PROBABLY SURE	POSITIVELY YES
My car will last me at least two more years.				
I am confident about my retirement plan.				
I have really good health coverage.				
I know where I plan to be living five years from now.				
I can name at least two friends who would bail me out of jail.				

■ Share with the group the statement you are most certain about. Would you describe yourself as a person who can live with a large amount of uncertainty, or a small amount of uncertainty?

■ Do you prefer to hang out with friends who are like you in the amount of uncertainty they can tolerate? Or would you rather be with someone who enjoys more or less certainty? Why?

Facts or Faith?

Consider this quote:

Alice laughed. "There's no use trying," she said. "One can't believe impossible things."

"I daresay you haven't had much practice," said the Queen. "When I was your age, I always did it for half-an-hour a day. Why, sometimes I've believed as many as six impossible things before breakfast." (Source: Alice in Wonderland *by Lewis Carroll. This version from www.sabian.org/Alice/lgchap05.htm.)*

■ Would you describe yourself as more like Alice or more like the Queen of Hearts?

■ What helps a person in dealing with uncertainty: facts, faith, practice, or something else?

STUDY

Read Mark 9:14-16.

1. Suggest what the scribes and disciples may have been arguing about.

2. Why do you suppose the crowd was "overwhelmed with awe" when they saw Jesus coming toward them?

Read Mark 9:17-21.

3. The father hadn't waited for Jesus but, instead, asked his disciples to cast out the evil spirit. Would you have done that? Why?

LEADER'S NOTES

There are some additional details given in the other Gospel accounts of this incident that you may want to point out. According to Matthew 17:14, 15, the father *knelt* before Jesus and begged, "Lord have mercy on my son." According to Luke 9:37-43: the boy was the man's only child; after the boy was healed, Jesus gave him back to the father; and the crowd was amazed at the greatness of God!

In the phrase "Help me overcome my unbelief!" (Mark 9:24), the Greek word translated "help" is a compound word formed from *boe* and *theo,* combining "cry out" and "run." The word vividly depicts a helper running toward one who is crying out for assistance. (Source: Archibald Robertson, *Word Pictures in the New Testament: Volume I* [Nashville, TN: Broadman Press, 1930], 342.)

4. In your opinion, who were the "faithless people" (v. 19) that Jesus was frustrated with? The crowd? The disciples who couldn't heal the boy? The teachers of the law who were arguing with the disciples?

5. Why do you think that Jesus asked the man how long his son had been tormented by the demon? Didn't Jesus already know?

6. Jesus didn't do many miracles in his hometown because of the people's lack of faith. (See Matthew 13:57, 58.) There didn't seem to be much faith in this locality either. What made this circumstance different? Why do you think Jesus chose to heal the boy, even though the father lacked certainty and the disciples lacked power?

Read Matthew 17:19, 20.

7. In this account of the incident, Jesus told his disciples that even faith as tiny as a mustard seed would enable them to accomplish impossible things. *There are so many reasons* not *to believe. Life can certainly test your certainty. If you aren't in the crucible now, you likely will be at some point. I don't want to be pessimistic, just truthful. Life is periodically hard, and it will attempt to break your resolve to trust God. (Unnamed,* p. 91)

What advice would you give to a person who wanted to increase his faith? Do you think the answer is different for different personality types or for people with different backgrounds? Why or why not?

ANOTHER UNCERTAIN HERO: JONAH

Jonah was certain that he *didn't* want to obey God's command to go to Nineveh. He was certain that a voyage to Tarshish would land him on the opposite end of the world from where God wanted him. When the huge storm arose, he was certain that God allowed the storm to punish him. He insisted that the sailors toss him overboard. After three days and nights inside the great fish, Jonah was finally *uncertain*.

Read Jonah's prayer in Jonah 2:1-9.

1. What phrases do you see that show his desperation?

2. What phrases indicate glimpses of faith?

3. What does Jonah have in common with the father of the demon-possessed boy in Mark 9?

APPLY

8. The emergency personnel who are prepared and on call to respond to trouble or disastrous situations are called first responders. Brainstorm a list of the various tasks that first responders might be expected to perform.

9. How is God himself the chief of all first responders? Read these verses. In what ways do they help you view God as eager to respond to you?

Psalm 86:5-7

Psalm 91:15

Luke 15:20

Romans 5:6-8

1 John 4:19

10. *He wanted to believe, chose to believe, and asked God's help for his uncertainty. Notice the role that he played in his own faith and the role that God played. He chose, God helped. An important step in a growing faith is to make this choice to ask for help, over and over, in as many circumstances as call for it. (Unnamed, p. 97)* The author suggests that the father in this account models for us the way to move through and out of uncertainty:

A. Invite God into your uncertainty.
B. Expect God to help.
C. Choose to act upon your faith however tiny it may be.
D. Begin again at step A.

Have you ever applied that sequence or a similar one in your own life? Share briefly your experience in moving through times of uncertainty. What hindered your progress? What helped you the most?

11. If the leader brought copies of lyrics for the song "Never Been Unloved" (or brought a laptop to look them up), read the lyrics now. Then discuss these questions: In what ways do you identify with the songwriter? Has uncertainty ever stopped you in your tracks, or at least slowed you down? What solution is offered in the song? Has that solution been effective in calming your own uncertainties? Why or why not?

12. "Lord, I believe, but help my unbelief about . . ."

Consider the circumstances you are currently facing. Is there a particular uncertainty you should ask the Lord to get involved in and give you assistance? As a group, read the phrase aloud together as a prayer, pausing for a brief moment for each person to silently fill in the blank with his or her own issue. Repeat this several times.

MORE THAN WORDS

You may be very ill, or caring for someone who is very ill, and your unanswered prayers may be shaking your confidence that God can or will do anything about it. (*Unnamed,* p. 92) Could your group give someone's faith a boost by doing something special for a family in your church or neighborhood who has a child with special needs? These parents seldom get an evening out because of the difficulties involved in finding a babysitter. Perhaps your group could provide dinner and child care for the children and give the parents a gift card to a local restaurant. Perhaps the family is swamped with doctor appointments and has no time or energy to paint their home or stain their deck. Contact them and ask the parents to let you know of their top three needs. Then, as a group, help meet at least one of those needs.

Before the next meeting read chapter 7 in *Unnamed.*

UNNOTICED

MARK 12:41-44

God sees the heart.

Noticed: observed, given polite or favorable attention, treated with civility, prominent, outstanding
Unnoticed: overlooked, ignored, inconspicuous, disregarded

THE BOTTOM LINE: *God calls us to do things and respond to needs in ways that may never be noticed by people. (Unnamed, p. 115)*

THE GOAL OF THIS SESSION is to increase our willingness to serve without recognition.

We will discover the delight God has toward those who are willing to serve him completely unnoticed and unrewarded.

We will rethink our attitudes about serving and giving and seek to find some creative ways to walk out the truths in our daily lives.

We will consider some ways in which we can serve and give to others in secret.

LEADER PREPARATION

Read Mark 12:41-44; Luke 18:9-14; Exodus 35:20-29; 36:4-7.

Review the questions and select the ones most appropriate for your group. You probably won't have time to discuss all of them.

Read chapter 7 in the book *Unnamed* by Chris Travis.

Pray for hearts to be softened toward a subject that can reveal a self-centered heart.

CONNECT
Anonymous Gifting and Re-gifting
- Have you ever received a gift from an anonymous donor? How did that make you feel? Did it drive you crazy not to know the source? Why or why not? Did it motivate you to "pay it forward" and give anonymously to someone else?
- Have you ever been re-gifted—you received someone else's leftover or unwanted gift? How did that make you feel? Have you ever given away something that someone else gave you? What was your motivation for doing so? Are there any gifts that are acceptable to re-gift? What about the gift of grace?

What's Your Tip Grade?
- How would you rate yourself as a tipper? (Check all that apply.)

  ____ I tend to be critical of the service so I can give less.
  ____ I sometimes resent having to pay more than the price of the meal.
  ____ I calculate the percentage to the penny.
  ____ I'd rather leave a religious tract.
  ____ I look forward to surprising my server by being generous.

■ Do you think tipping reveals more about the tipper or more about the service rendered? Why?

■ Those who enjoy tipping generously can tell, if willing, how they developed that habit and why they enjoy doing that.

STUDY

Read Mark 12:41-44.

LEADER'S NOTES

Don't be surprised at the emotion and strong opinions that may emerge during this session. When the topic includes money, people react strongly.

Tithing—giving 10 percent of one's income to God—is not commanded in the New Testament. The commands are focused on surrendering one's whole life to God and being a good (generous) manager of everything God has given.

1. Try to imagine yourself in the shoes of the widow spoken of in this account. Why do you suppose she brought all that she had? What might have motivated her?

Read Mark 12:38-40.

2. What particular warning did Jesus make against the religious leaders that revealed their attitude toward widows? How do you think they would "cheat widows out of their property"? How did the leaders attempt to make up for that practice?

Read Luke 18:9-14.

3. Compare the two participants in this scene with the two categories of givers Jesus spoke about in Mark 12:43, 44.

Read Exodus 35:20-29.

4. How did the Israelites react to God's command (back in verse 5) to bring an offering? Find at least two characteristics of the givers.

5. What theme was repeated in verse 29?

Read Exodus 36:4-7.

6. Why couldn't the people bring more? Have you ever been part of a church where this command was given? What happened?

7. *So how do we go unnoticed day in and day out and maintain our drive and joy in serving?* (*Unnamed*, p. 109) Look in these Scriptures to discover encouragement for continuing to serve and give to others without recognition or notice.

Hebrews 6:10

Matthew 10:42

Proverbs 19:17

Revelation 14:13

ANOTHER UNNOTICED HERO: THE PASSOVER HOST

Read Mark 14:10-16. (See also Matthew 26:14-19; Luke 22:4-13.)

1. In Mark 14:13 what clue was to lead the disciples to the right house?

2. What message was to be given to the homeowner? (v. 14)

3. Based on verses 10 and 11, why do you think Jesus gave these instructions in such a mysterious way?

4. What signs of Jesus' supernatural knowledge are in this account?

5. Matthew 26:18 notes that the homeowner was to be told that Jesus said, "My time has come." What might the homeowner and disciples have thought he meant? What do you think he meant?

No other details are given about the homeowner. He willingly opened a room to Jesus and his disciples, but nothing indicates that the host was present or participated in the meal—a history-making meal that instituted the Lord's Supper. He donated the space, but he did not intrude. This generous but unnoticed man quietly played a significant role in Jesus' final hours, as Jesus steadily and purposefully moved forward to complete his mission on earth.

APPLY

8. Individuals learn about and grow in the grace of giving in different ways. What has motivated you? Which of the "inspirations" listed below might increase your generosity? (Check all that apply.)

___ Seeing a deep need
___ Seeing the generosity of another person
___ God's commands to give generously
___ Recognizing your own need to let go of your stuff
___ Getting out of debt (freeing up your resources so you can redirect them for God's purposes)
___ Other _____

9. Why do you think the preferred method for giving, praying, and fasting in Matthew 6:2-6, 16-18 is in secrecy?

10. What delights God about private acts such as these?

11. Consider these possible motives people have for giving:

- Feeling blessed by God and wanting to give back
- Wanting to be noticed for being generous
- Desiring to "atone" for doing something wrong
- Wanting to pay God back for something nice that he did
- Feeling compelled; others might think badly of the giver otherwise

Is it better not to give if you don't have the right motive? What does that say about your heart? Is it possible to improve your heart while not practicing generosity? Explain your response.

12. Discuss the following scenarios:

- A minister's family decides that they have so much, they don't need any more gifts. They opt to re-gift every gift that they receive from their congregation at Christmas time. They pass on treats, gift cards, and ornaments to families they know who are in need. How much criticism do you think they might receive? Will they be labeled ungrateful?
- Some friends decide that they don't need to keep giving each other birthday cards and gifts. They donate to a charity chosen by the birthday person. What would happen if you suggested that idea to your group of friends?
- Volunteers who sort clothing and other items for collections to be sent to missionaries say that the majority of donations received are not in acceptable condition. What could be done to change the expectation so that people would be excited to donate new or nearly new items instead of getting rid of their trash and junk?
- A church member says, "My family already tithes. I don't really like being asked to contribute more to special causes. It seems they are always taking an offering for a mission project or local charity. Don't I give enough already?"

MORE THAN WORDS
Fast for Food

If we aren't going without something in order to give, are we really giving? (*Unnamed*, p. 113) One church challenged their members to give up some food-related item for a month: specialty coffee, a fast-food meal, a candy bar, or eating out. Families saved their money and brought it for a special offering at the end of the month. The offering was given to a local food bank. This "Fast for Food" theme proved much more effective than having each family bring a few cans of food each week.

Choose to fast from something you enjoy. Plan to give it up for a month. Don't wait until the end of the month to try to come up with the money. Put it in a change jar or dresser drawer every day or every week. Then pool your group's savings and donate to a local food bank.

You Can't Talk About It

Divide into three groups. Each group can brainstorm possible acts of kindness that an individual or possibly your group could do covertly, without being noticed or taking credit.

Group 1: random kindness to strangers
Group 2: secret service at the church building
Group 3: good deeds in a neighborhood or for a neighbor

After about five minutes of brainstorming, each group can briefly share their ideas.

Then determine to secretly assist someone. Commit that service to God. Don't speak about your good deed to anyone but God (and any group members involved).

Before the next meeting read chapter 8 in *Unnamed*.

UNRANKED

ACTS 23:12-24

If you fear God, you need fear nothing else.

> **Ranked:** having status, social class, or position; privileged
> **Unranked:** lacking recognition, without status, unimportant

THE BOTTOM LINE: Fear can become merely a small hindrance when viewed from the perspective of God's plan and God's power.

THE GOAL OF THIS SESSION is to diminish the fears that intimidate, trap, and keep us from living as God intended.

We will realize that fear of God frees us from all other fears.

We will consider ways to conquer our own fears.

LEADER PREPARATION

Read Acts 23:12-24.

Read chapter 8 in the book *Unnamed* by Chris Travis.

Have plenty of index cards for the opening activities and for question 12.

Pray that your group will recognize the ways fears hold you back from accomplishing God's will. Pray for openness to allow God to deal with those fears.

CONNECT
Guess Who's a Scaredy-Cat?

- What is something you dread? On the index cards distributed by the group facilitator, write down something you currently are or used to be afraid of. Gather all the cards together and mix them up. Read them aloud one at a time. Group members should try to guess who wrote each one.
- If you wrote about a past fear, what helped you overcome that fear?
- If you are a parent, how have you helped your children deal with fears?

Top Fears

- What fears would you say are the most common? Jot down on an index card what you believe are the top three fears of most people. Have someone in your group collect the cards and tally the results.
- If this survey were conducted in another country, do you think the fears listed would be different? Why or why not?
- Should a Christian's list of fears be different from those of a nonbeliever? Why or why not?

STUDY

Read Acts 23:12-24.

1. *You may have had some enemies in the past. I'm sure there are people out there who don't care for me. But Paul's enemies played in a whole different league.* (*Unnamed*, p. 124) What did the assassins want the chief priests to do?

2. Why were the Romans careful to protect Paul? (See Acts 22:25-29.)

3. Why do you suppose Paul didn't ask to see the commander himself? Why did he rely on his nephew to explain the plot?

4. How accurately do you think Paul's nephew reported to the commander what he had heard? Did he exaggerate? Did he leave anything out? Support your answer.

5. What reason could there be for the commander's willingness to listen to the boy instead of ignoring or dismissing him?

6. How many total soldiers were deployed to guard Paul?

LEADER'S NOTES

The conspirators who took an oath to kill Paul were saying, "Let us be cursed if we don't accomplish this." The word used is *anathema*. The same word is used in Mark 14:71 to describe Peter calling curses down upon himself when he denied Jesus. (Source: Archibald Robertson, *Word Pictures in the New Testament: Volume III* [Nashville, TN: Broadman Press, 1930], 403.)

This plot against Paul is an example of Jesus' prediction in John 16:2: "Those who kill you will think they are doing a holy service for God."

The commander actually included his own name, Claudius Lysias, in the letter he wrote to the governor. (See Acts 23:26.)

 ANOTHER UNRANKED HERO: JAHAZIEL

Read 2 Chronicles 20:5-26.

1. Jehoshaphat, king of Judah, was facing an attack from three enemy armies. What was his attitude about the circumstance, according to 2 Chronicles 20:6, 9, and 12?

2. His adviser, Jahaziel, received a message from the Spirit of God. What instruction did Jahaziel deliver to the army of Judah in verse 17?

3. What famous desperate situation might have been brought to Jehoshaphat's mind by Jahaziel's urging to "stand still and watch"? (See Exodus 14:13.)

4. What did Jahaziel's words prompt King Jehoshaphat to do in preparation for the battle? (vv. 18, 19)

5. Who did the king appoint to lead the army into battle in verse 21? What did these men employ as their weapon?

6. How did the battle turn out? (vv. 22-26)

King Jehoshaphat deserves much credit for his faith and courage. It would have been an embarrassing defeat had the enemy armies charged right through the front-line singers. But it was the urgent and confident plea of the little-known Jahaziel that set things in motion for King Jehoshaphat to face his fears.

APPLY

7. Using the letters below, create an acrostic. Each word or phrase should suggest an action step toward overcoming fear. Group members might prefer to work in pairs to come up with ideas.

N

O

F

E

A

R

8. *When we have a proper reverence, respect, and fear of the Lord, it frees us from fear of anything else. (Unnamed, p. 128)* What advice would you give to a new believer who asked you what it means to have a proper fear of the Lord and how to develop that reverence?

Read Jeremiah 5:21-23.

9. How does God describe the people who refuse to fear him?

10. Why is it reasonable to fear God? (See Jeremiah 10:7.)

11. What are some benefits of fearing God? (See Proverbs 1:7; Ecclesiastes 12:13, 14.)

12. Children in Sunday school often learn Psalm 56:3 as a beginner verse for dealing with fear: "When I am afraid, I will trust in you" (*NIV*). Review the following verses. Share with the group which one inspires you the most and why. Print it on an index card and place it where you can see it daily, until you have transferred its encouragement to your heart.

Psalm 34:4

Psalm 34:9

Isaiah 35:4

Isaiah 41:10

Romans 8:15

13. What in today's discussion has motivated or encouraged you to take a step to deal with your own personal fears?

MORE THAN WORDS

Take time to individually complete this activity. Review the bulleted "If I . . ." list on page 123 of *Unnamed.* If you were making a similar list for yourself, what would you include? Select one of your worst case scenarios to offer to God. Tell God that you are still more than fearful about this situation but you are laying your fears before him. Invite him to work in your heart. Commit to following the steps he puts in front of you.

Go back and skim through the challenges and ideas in the More Than Words sections at the end of each session of this study. Select one that you will accept as a challenge to get out of your comfort zone.

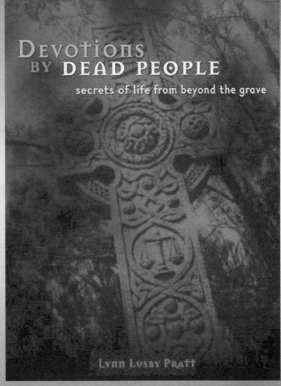